Journey of a Toy

John Malam

Raintree

www.raintreepublishers.co.uk

Visit our website to find out more information about Raintree books.

To order:

☎ Phone 0845 6044371
🖷 Fax +44 (0) 1865 312263
✉ Email myorders@raintreepublishers.co.uk

Customers from outside the UK please telephone +44 1865 312262

Raintree is an imprint of Capstone Global Library Limited, a company incorporated in England and Wales having its registered office at 7 Pilgrim Street, London, EC4V 6LB – Registered company number: 6695582

Edited by Dan Nunn and Diyan Leake
Designed by Cynthia Della-Rovere
Original illustrations © Capstone Global Library Ltd 2012
Illustrated by Capstone Global Library Ltd
Picture research by Mica Brancic
Production by Alison Parsons
Originated by Capstone Global Library Ltd
Printed and bound in China by Leo Paper Products Ltd

ISBN 978 1 406 23937 9 (hardback)
16 15 14 13 12
10 9 8 7 6 5 4 3 2 1

British Library Cataloguing in Publication Data
Malam, John, 1957–
  Journey of a toy.
  688.7'2-dc22
A full catalogue record for this book is available from the British Library.

Acknowledgements
The author and publishers are grateful to the following for permission to reproduce copyright material: Alamy p. 28 (© Picture Press/Jürco Börner); Getty Images pp. 8 (© AFP Photo/Michael Cizek), 13 (© The Washington Post/Katherine Frey), 19 (© Universal Images Group), 21 (© AFP Photo/Michal Cizek), 22 (© Bloomberg/Vladimir Weiss), 26 (© Bloomberg/Vladimir Weiss), 27 (Bloomberg/Vladimir Weiss); PA p. 9 (© The Washington Post/Mark Gail); Science Photo Library pp. 16 (© Maximilian Stock Ltd), 17 (© Philippe Psaila), 18 (© Klaus Guldbrandsen), 20 (© Volker Steger); Shutterstock pp. 1 (© Nataliya Hora), 3 (© A. Gorohov), 4 (© Losevsky Pavel), 5 top left (© Robert Wolkaniec), 5 bottom left (© Fedorov Oleksiy), 5 right (© Terekhov Igor), 6 (© Andrea Danti), 7 (© cobalt88), 10 (© Goodluz), 11 (computer screen, © OtnaYdur), 11 (3D truck, © Tim Arbaev), 14 (© Freerk Brouwer), 15 (© Nataliya Hora), 23 (© Dmitry Kalinovsky), 24 (© Anyka), 25 (© Sascha Burkard), 29 left (© Coprid), 29 right (© AGorohov), 31 top (© Andrea Danti), 31 middle (© Freerk Brouwer), 31 bottom (© Sascha Burkard); SuperStock p. 12 (© Blend Images).

Cover photographs of a small replica of an excavator (© A. Gorohov) and industrial plastic granules (© Coprid) reproduced with permission of Shutterstock.

Every effort has been made to contact copyright holders of material reproduced in this book. Any omissions will be rectified in subsequent printings if notice is given to the publisher.

Contents

Some words are shown in bold, **like this**. You can find out what they mean by looking in the Glossary.

What will you play with today?

Have you ever wondered what your toys are made from? Many of them are made from plastic. Plastic is a very useful material. It can be **moulded** into shapes and used to make lots of different things.

It's fun to choose a new toy to play with.

Plastic things can
be very colourful.

Plastic is everywhere. Toothbrushes, combs,
rulers, pencil pots, and school dinner trays
are all made from plastic. Turn the page to
find out about the journey of a plastic toy.

Making plastic

Plastic is made in **factories**. It is made from **chemicals** found in oil. Oil is a thick, runny **liquid**. It comes from deep under ground and beneath the sea.

Plastic toys start out as oil.

There are a lot of machines and pipes at an oil refinery.

Oil is pumped along pipes to oil **refineries**. It may be carried by huge ships called tankers. At the refineries, oil is made into petrol. It is also made into the chemicals used to make plastic.

Ideas for new plastic toys

A new toy made from plastic starts when someone has a good idea. Many new ideas come from people called **product designers**. They work for companies that make toys.

This product designer is working on a new toy.

These children are testing a new toy for playing music.

Children also have ideas for new toys. Product designers talk to children to find out what toys they would like to play with.

Making drawings

Product designers make lots of drawings for the new toy. First, they make the drawings on paper. Then they put the best drawings on to a computer.

These designers are working on an idea for a new toy.

The computer drawings look three-dimensional (3D). This means they do not look flat. 3D drawings look like they have depth.

Drawings made on a computer look just like the finished toy.

Does it work?

It is very important to find out if the new toy works and if children like it. The toy company makes a few **samples** of the toy. Some lucky children get to play with the samples. The **product designers** see how the children play with the toy.

Samples of new toys are tested before lots of them are made.

Children play with toys and have ideas for new ones.

The people from the toy company ask the children lots of questions. They find out what children like about the toy. They find out what the children do not like. It helps them to make a really good toy.

Little bits of plastic

Plastic toys are made in **factories**. Some plastic toys start off as little bits of plastic called **granules**. The granules come in different colours.

Plastic granules can be all sorts of colours.

A special type of plastic is used to make toys. It is hard and shiny and has a very long name. People call it ABS for short.

ABS is short for acrylonitrile butadiene styrene. No wonder most people just call it ABS!

Melting and moulding

The little **granules** of plastic are heated up. They turn from a **solid** into a **liquid**. The liquid plastic is thick and gooey. It is very, very hot.

The liquid plastic goes into machines like these to be made into the shape of the toys.

This machine has moulds for making plastic bricks.

Next, the liquid plastic is poured into **moulds**. A toy might have many parts. It will need lots of moulds to make them all.

Cooling down

The **liquid** plastic cools down quickly. As it cools, it changes from a liquid into a **solid**. The parts of the toy become completely hard very soon.

The new parts are dropped into a bin.

This machine can count out the plastic parts.

The plastic parts come out of the **moulds**. They go into bins on a **conveyor belt**. It takes them to other parts of the toy **factory**.

Painting and joining

Some parts need painting. A **conveyor belt** carries these parts to a painting machine. It sprays paint on to the parts to add patterns. It also paints eyes, hair, and smiles.

The arms and legs are still to be joined on to this toy.

People in the **factory** put together some parts of a toy.

Finally, all the parts of the toy are joined together. This is done by an **assembly machine**. Some parts snap into place. Other parts are held in place by tiny screws.

Toy boxes and cartons

The finished toy is put into a box. The box is very colourful. It has the name of the toy on it. It says what the toy is like. The box might have a see-through plastic window, so you can see the toy inside.

A box that toys come in will have pictures and other information on it.

Cartons are stacked inside a warehouse.

The toy boxes are put into large cardboard boxes called cartons. Each carton holds a lot of toy boxes. The cartons are sealed and put into a **warehouse**.

Carried by ship

Plastic toys are made in many countries. They need to be sent to the places where they will be sold. Lorries transport the cartons of toys from the toy **factory** to a **port** on the coast of the country where they are made.

This ship is at a port.

At the port, the cartons are loaded into big metal boxes called **containers**. The containers hold hundreds of cartons. They are put on to a **cargo ship**. The ship takes the containers to the countries where they are needed.

Into the shops

It might take a few weeks for the **cargo ship** to sail to your country. When it does, the **containers** of toys are unloaded. Then they are sent to shops where they are put on sale.

This worker is putting toys on the shelves in a shop.

Shoppers take the toys to the checkout to pay for them.

People pay the shops for the toys. The shops pay the **factory** that made the toys. The toy factory pays the factory that made the plastic **granules**. The granule factory pays the oil company that pumped the oil from the ground.

A present for you!

Isn't it great to be given a toy as a present? You can't wait to take the wrapping paper off, open the box, and start playing with your new toy!

Each toy you play with has been on a long journey.

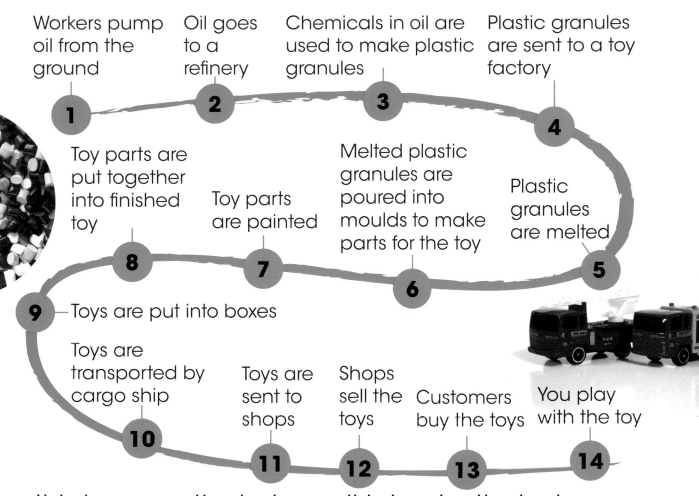

1. Workers pump oil from the ground
2. Oil goes to a refinery
3. Chemicals in oil are used to make plastic granules
4. Plastic granules are sent to a toy factory
5. Plastic granules are melted
6. Melted plastic granules are poured into moulds to make parts for the toy
7. Toy parts are painted
8. Toy parts are put together into finished toy
9. Toys are put into boxes
10. Toys are transported by cargo ship
11. Toys are sent to shops
12. Shops sell the toys
13. Customers buy the toys
14. You play with the toy

It takes months to turn oil into plastic, but it only takes a few days to change plastic **granules** into finished toys. Just think, somewhere in the world oil is being pumped from the ground right now. That oil might become a toy that you play with.

Glossary

assembly machine machine that joins pieces together

cargo ship ship that carries goods. The goods are called cargo.

chemical one of the materials that makes up another material

container large metal box filled with cargo

conveyor belt rubber surface that moves along, carrying things on it

factory building where things are made

granule small grain of something

liquid material that flows, such as water

mould hollow container that makes objects the same shape as itself

port place where ships sail to and from

product designer person who decides how something should look and work

refinery factory that turns a raw material into something useful

sample example of something to show what it looks like

solid material that is hard and keeps its shape

warehouse building where things are stored

Toy quiz

1. What is plastic made from?
   (see page 6)

2. What are little bits of plastic called?
   (see page 14)

3. When plastic granules are heated up, what happens to them?
   (see page 16)

4. What does an assembly machine do? (see page 21)

5. What are big metal boxes on cargo ships called? (see page 25)

Find out more

See a short slide show of how Lego bricks are made: **images.businessweek.com/ss/06/11/1129_makingof_lego/index_01.htm**

Click on the "Materials" box to find out about plastic and other materials: **www.bbc.co.uk/schools/ks2bitesize/science**

Answers

1. chemicals found in oil, 2. granules, 3. They become a liquid, 4. It joins all the parts together, 5. containers

Index